CW00725087

Winning

business plans

Polly Bird

flash.

Hodder Education
338 Euston Road, London NW1 3BH.

Hodder Education is an Hachette UK company

First published in UK 2011 by Hodder Education.

British Library Cataloguing in Publication Data: a catalogue record for this title
is available from the British Library.

10 9 8 7 6 5 4 3 2 1

The publisher has used its best endeavours to ensure that any website
addresses referred to in this book are correct and active at the time of going
to press. However, the publisher and the author have no responsibility for the
websites and can make no guarantee that a site will remain live or that the
content will remain relevant, decent or appropriate.

The publisher has made every effort to mark as such all words which it
believes to be trademarks. The publisher should also like to make it clear that
the presence of a word in the book, whether marked or unmarked, in no way
affects its legal status as a trademark.

Every reasonable effort has been made by the publisher to trace the copyright
holders of material in this book. Any errors or omissions should be notified in
writing to the publisher, who will endeavour to rectify the situation for any
reprints and future editions.

Hachette UK's policy is to use papers that are natural, renewable and
recyclable products and made from wood grown in sustainable forests.
The logging and manufacturing processes are expected to conform to the
environmental regulations of the country of origin.

www.hoddereducation.co.uk

Typeset by MPS Limited, a Macmillan Company.
Printed in Great Britain by CPI Cox & Wyman, Reading.

Contents

1

why you need a business plan

Whether you have already started a business or intend to start one soon, you need a business plan. A business plan is an important business tool. It is a document that describes your business in detail and shows short- and long-term issues. It is a guide for future action as well as a means of showing potential backers that your business is viable. Whether you write the plan alone or with colleagues it needs to be created with the intended audience in mind. Before you begin, work out what skills you or your colleagues will need so that you are aware of any potential gaps in the plan. You will need to keep your plan updated so that you know how your business is progressing and what changes, if any, need to be made. Remember, the content of your plan will only be as good as the information put into it.

A business plan is a document that describes your business in detail and suggests how it might progress in the future. It shows what actions need to be taken immediately and which are long-term issues. It is therefore something that can not only be used for a short-term situation, such as raising finance for a particular project, but also as a guide to how the business should progress. It normally contains information about what the business is, how it will operate, how the product or service will be marketed and the present and future financial position. It shows what the business can do and what you want the business to do in the future.

Each plan will be tailored to the specific business or proposed business being considered and will vary according to the importance of the situation. One thing is clear: people who make business plans are more successful than those who don't because they have a better understanding of their business and how they want their business to develop. Time taken to prepare a business plan is never wasted.

There are two main types of plan. First, a short-term plan aimed at getting a loan, investment, grant or other kind of aid. Second, a long-term plan that will help you develop your business and provide a blueprint for progress that will motivate staff and guide managers. Both types of plan have the same basic core of vital information, but a short-term plan will focus on the need for financial help while the long-term plan will provide more information about the business's long-term aims. In practice, the difference between the two is more to do with length and emphasis than content. Any plan should contain enough information to explain the business in enough detail to encourage investors or lenders and that in itself is the basis for long-term planning.

Uses of a business plan

There are many reasons for producing a business plan and some or all of them will apply to your business.
* **Obtaining financial backing.** Both new and existing businesses can have a need for money, and a business plan

will show why investing in your business will be profitable. Your local trade and business organizations will be able to give advice about getting started with your business. Try contacting your local Business Link or local Enterprise agencies. There are also government organizations and other agencies – public, private and voluntary – that can provide advice and help for new and existing businesses.

* **Showing that a new business is viable.** If you are starting a new business, your plan will show potential backers what your business involves and that it will pay. It will show how likely the business is to succeed and reassure investors or lenders that the business will not go bankrupt and will make a profit. Anyone providing financial assistance will need to know that your business can repay any money and can sustain interest payments.

* **Helping people become self-employed.** Anyone wishing to become self-employed should produce a business plan whether they need immediate financial assistance or not. Not only will it concentrate thinking on how the business will work and highlight potential problems, but it will show whether working for oneself is a practical option.

* **Discovering strengths and weaknesses.** By writing a business plan you can see where there are potential or existing problems as well as where the strengths of the business lie. For example, compiling a business plan might highlight a lack of certain skills in managers or employees. A useful tool for this is the SWOT analysis which will be explained in Chapter 3.

* **Encouraging partners.** A good business plan will encourage people to join you as partners in your business. It will show that they will be taking part in a venture with a future.

* **Guiding employees.** The plan can be used to show employees the direction of the business and to enlist their help with the plan's execution. It can also be used to keep employees informed of changes and therefore boost their morale.

* **Helping you make decisions.** With the detailed information about your business at your fingertips, you can make informed decisions quickly and confidently. You will be able to make better decisions immediately, rather than have to gather the background information once the problem has arisen.
* **Blueprint for future action.** A good business plan provides an ongoing guide to how the business should progress. It helps you manage the business efficiently and is a map for progress.
* **Improving internal management communication.** The better understanding managers have of the business the better they can communicate between departments. Managers need to know how the business works on a day-to-day basis. A business plan will show up any badly managed areas of an existing business or potential managerial problems for a new business.
* **Pinpointing areas for development.** Writing a plan can highlight areas which it would be profitable to develop.
* **Highlighting problems.** The plan will not only show where immediate problems need dealing with but will show where future problems might occur. This will help reduce a 'fire-fighting' approach to problems and therefore save time, energy and money.
* **Planning resources.** Your plan will enable you to see what resources you need and be able to plan for them. You should therefore not be caught unawares by lack of resources at any future point.
* **Getting ahead of the competition.** Any business plan needs to demonstrate an understanding of your competitors and their strengths and weaknesses. By researching this you will have a plan that gives you the tools to market your product or service in ways that will overcome competition.
* **Making the best use of what is available.** Even if your business does not have everything that ideally it should have,

by creating a plan you will be able to see clearly what its assets are and so be able to make the best use of them.

* **Analysing the viability of a new product or service.** Creating a business plan gives you the opportunity to research the viability of a new product or service and to see how it will fit into the prevailing business market. A plan will help you uncover any previously unnoticed flaws in the processes of creating a product or service and getting it onto the market.
* **Providing a personal long-term guide to progress.** By referring to the plan you can see where the business is deviating from this and make adjustments accordingly. It can also be a motivational tool by demonstrating where and when your business has progressed according to the plan.
* **Providing an overall view of the business.** You might be so closely involved in your business that you do not see the overall picture. Preparing a business plan will make this clearer and provide an overview.
* **Concentrating your thinking.** A business plan will make you think carefully about your ideas and view them as other people will see them. It will enable you to solve problems that the plan throws up before readers see it.
* **Impressing buyers.** This is an overlooked reason for providing a business plan, but potential buyers of a business will want reassurance that the business is viable and is likely to continue making a profit. It will also give them a detailed breakdown of how the business operates.
* **Getting regulatory approval.** If your business will require approval from a regulatory body then the plan will show the body that the business meets all the necessary criteria.

Preparing your plan

You should share the business plan with your work colleagues or employees. If they understand how the business is supposed to work and progress they will be encouraged to help the process. They might also have suggestions about ways to improve on the procedures and product or service. Advice from people who have first-hand experience of the way your business actually works is invaluable. If you are intending to start a business and have potential partners or employees then you can show the plan to them.

Your bank manager, grants providers and investors will want to see evidence that you understand the product or service you sell and that you have carefully evaluated the prospects of your business. You might also show your plan to business advice organizations so that they can help you improve it or give other advice.

When you know who will see the plan you will be able to tailor its content and presentation to their needs.

Obviously, you are the best person to write your business plan. It can often work well if you join forces with your employees or business partners. There are advantages in preparing your business plan yourself. First, you will most likely be presenting it to a lender or investor yourself. If you have prepared the plan you will know the contents better than anyone else. You will be able to play up the strengths of the proposal. Second, you can see which sections need fine-tuning and can adjust them accordingly. By doing this yourself you can quickly adapt the plan to changing needs.

It is sensible to prepare at least a first draft yourself, if you can, and then get an expert to prepare a suitable final version. A first draft ensures that you get the ideas that you consider important down on paper. It gives you a basis for discussion with a professional who can bring an objective eye to it.

You might decide that you would prefer a professional business plan writer or someone else to prepare the plan for you. An accountant or a business consultant, given the relevant information, will create a business plan for you but they will charge for doing so. If you are starting a new business this may well be too expensive for you. There are also a number of individuals and agencies who provide a business plan preparation service.

There are computer programs to help with the creation of a business plan but they cannot write the plan for you.

The internet as a research tool

The internet is now the first place to look for information. Many businesses, companies, banks, government bodies, trade associations and other organizations have a web presence with their own websites containing much useful information. However, there are risks with using internet information alone. Anyone can post information on the internet so you need to ensure that you access reliable sites. Websites produced by well-known organizations will be reliable. If you don't know the company's reputation, check their details in a yearbook or trade directory at your local library or phone their industry body. Check that information is up-to-date by looking for the date that the website was updated. Look for contact details and check the names of the organization's owners. Look at the press section of the site, if there is one, and see when the latest release was produced. This is a good place to find the latest company news.

Starting actions

Here are a few ideas to help you get ready to do the necessary research to write your plan:

1 Make a list of all the organizations, people and other possible sources of information. You can add to this as you get ideas from reading this book.
2 Create a timetable for making contact or doing desk research.
3 Keep a note of references and contact numbers as you go along.
4 Sort your research into broad categories as you go along – use the chapter headings in this book to help you.

You now know what a business plan is and why you need one. You should also have a clear idea of your intended audience and which skills you or your colleagues need to acquire. Now you are ready to start creating your plan.

2

what type of business?

You need to be clear about whether you are offering a product or service and what kind of legal format your business will take. You also need to decide whether you need to deal with such things as registering a trademark or company name, taking out a patent or safeguarding copyright or design. Consider whether other types of business set-up such as a consultancy or franchise might be a more suitable way of operating your business. Ensure that you are clear enough about your main business idea to be able to describe it in a few sentences and that you can put up any financial security required by lenders or investors. You need to focus on the key objectives of your business. This will help you focus your research for your business plan. Once you are clear about your business idea and business objectives you can start writing them down.

Types of business ownership

In your business plan you will need to provide details about the legal ownership of your business. Any potential lender, investor, grant provider or anyone who might offer other kinds of help will want to know that you have the legal right to be negotiating with them and that your business is, or will be, created in accordance with the correct legal procedures.

There are several kinds of business ownership and each has its benefits and problems.

Sole trader

This is a common type of small business ownership. The business is owned and operated by one individual. If you run a business on these lines you get all the profits and are liable for all the debts. Your trading name and address must appear on all documents. You need to tell the Inland Revenue and Social Security the date that you started working for yourself and the date you actually started trading. You do not, however, have to publish your accounts.

Partnership

Two or more individuals together form a partnership of between two and twenty members. Each partner has a liability for all debts. You don't have to have a contract drawn up but it is sensible to ensure that you have an agreement about issues that might cause conflict, such as what happens if all the partners disagree on an issue, how much investment each partner must make in the business and what is the procedure to be followed if one partner wants to leave the business. A solicitor can advise you of the best means of doing this. Partners can be active or sleeping. Sleeping partners invest in the business but do not take part in its day-to-day running. They are only liable for the amount of their initial investment. At least one partner must be a general partner with unlimited liability for all the debts of the partnership.

Limited company

This is a difficult business type to set up. Once a limited company has been set up it becomes a legal entity entirely separate from whoever owns it. The individuals who own it are not liable for anything except the shares that they have. The company must pay corporation tax on any profits and PAYE and National Insurance for its employees. Directors and employees must pay class one insurance and have National Insurance and tax deducted from their salaries. Limited companies can be public or private. This is a decision your accountant can help you make depending on the type of business you have.

Other business types

There are other types of businesses that you might want to consider.

Consultancy

This is a business where you are offering your service to others as an expert in your field. It can be run by one person (the consultant) or can be a business in which more than one consultant is available to provide the service.

Co-operative

When many people band together to operate a business on an equal footing, it is known as a co-operative. Everyone puts the same amount of time and money into the business, works and reaps the benefit equally.

Franchise

A franchise is a popular way of starting in a business. You buy the rights to trade under the parent company name and in return get a business already run on a proven successful idea. You pay the franchiser a royalty fee based on your sales. Although nearly three-quarters of all new businesses fail, most franchises are successful. Most franchisers provide training, advice and, where applicable, contacts as well as supplying the basic stock.

Choosing a trading name

If you are a sole trader you may want to trade under your own name. If you want to use a trade name and perhaps a logo you should apply to register the design of the logo as a trademark and check that the name you want to use is not controlled. If, as a sole trader, you want to trade under another name you must still ensure that your own name appears on all documents related to your business sent out to the public.

If you decide to set up a limited company, you will need to register it at Companies House. You will need to provide Companies House, and the people you deal with, with certain information for the record. There are four main types of company:

* private, limited by shares
* private, limited by guarantee
* private unlimited
* public limited company (PLC).

For the purposes of this book the private limited company is likely to be the one kind you might consider at the moment. You need to provide a memorandum of association detailing the company name, the address of the registered office and what it will do. You also need to provide articles of association which set out the rules for how the company's internal affairs will be run. A private company must have at least one director and one secretary and must make annual accounts available. For further information look at the Companies House website.

Protecting your business idea

Depending on what kinds of products or services your business will be dealing with, you will probably want to know how you can protect your trading name, logo, designs or creative work. Protecting your original ideas will be important to you, and the business should be protected against copying or 'passing off'. There are several ways you can do this.

Detailed information about means of protection can be found at the website of the UK Patent Office.

Registering a patent

A patent is granted by the government to an inventor and protects how your idea works. It gives you ownership of the invention and the right to prevent other people from making, using or selling it. If you have invented the better mousetrap (and many people think they have) you need to protect it from exploitation by others by applying for a patent from the UK Patent Office. Applying for a patent is not straightforward. You have to supply several detailed documents and you might want to employ a patent procurer to ensure that your application is completed correctly.

Registering a trademark

Your trademark is a sign that distinguishes your products and services from anyone else's. It might include any combination of words, symbols or pictures. Even if you have registered your business name at Companies House, it does not mean that your trademark is also protected so you need to register your trademark separately.

Registering a design

If you have created a product that has a new and individual character in either its form or decoration then you might be able to register it. This can be done through the UK Patent Office.

Protecting copyright

If your business will involve producing original writing, artwork or other creative work then your work is automatically protected in the UK. Musical, dramatic, literary or artistic work is protected for 70 years after the death of the author. You do not need to use a copyright symbol. Although your copyright will probably be protected in most places abroad, this is not invariably so. There is no way of proving originality of your work except by arguing it in court in the case of supposed infringement of copyright. Some people deposit a copy of their work in a bank or with a solicitor. However, if you think your copyright is infringed, bear in mind legal costs. It might well be quicker and cheaper to sort out the problem with the infringer.

You need to work out early on whether you will be providing products or services and whether you will be selling them directly to your customers or indirectly. Generally you can divide these into several types:

* product sold directly to customer (e.g. in shops)
* products sold indirectly to customer (e.g. to wholesaler)
* services with personal customer contact (e.g. alternative healer)
* services with distant contact with customers (e.g. telephone secretarial services).

Until you know what kind of service or product you will offer you will not be able to write your business plan.

You no doubt already have your business idea. Now is the time to think about exactly what kind of business you will be running. Will it require employees, retail outlets, a mail order service, a website? Or perhaps you intend to offer a service in people's homes or do everything for your customers yourself in your own home?

The main business idea that you put in your business plan should be related to the type of business that you have or intend to have. You need to describe how the business is or will be set up and its main purpose. To do this you need to explain its key objectives.

Focusing on key objectives

Closely associated with your main business idea is the need to focus on the key objectives of your business and how you see your business idea fitting in with them. In your plan you need to focus on the key objectives, that is the main aims for your business. Ask yourself:

* what do I want the business to achieve?
* what are my goals for the business?
* how will my business idea contribute to the main goals of my business?

When you have the answers to these questions you will be better prepared to focus your research for your business idea. A plan that can demonstrate clearly a well thought-out and focused business idea that fits in with the main aims of the business has a better chance of success.

The key goals of your business will be closely related to why you want to establish the business (apart from the money). Is it fame, a chance to change the world, to be the best in the business? Whatever it is it, you need to make sure that you are clear about your business aims and where your idea fits in with it.

Before you take the next step and go ahead with your business idea you need to consider whether you can afford to take the financial risks necessary to get started. Unless you have enough capital of your own to proceed, you will have to approach lenders or investors and this will involve putting up security. You need to decide whether you can afford to do this.

To raise money from a long-term lender or venture capitalists you will need to put up security. You need to decide whether your business will be sound enough to take the risk of putting up your home as security. If you have a family it is something you need to discuss with your partner. After all, if the business fails and you lose the property, so does your family.

Investors of capital will want something from a business such as limited control of it or a percentage of the profits equal to a percentage of ownership. Before they will consider investing their money they will want to be convinced that the business is or will be financially viable and likely to provide them with a reasonable return on their investment. They will also require a get-out clause so that they can withdraw if the business fails, or looks like failing.

You might be able to arrange an initial loan by means of equity capital without interest and agree that it will be repaid when the business is a success. It is not a good idea to get a bank loan to do this because a bank might decide to recall the loan before you are ready to do so.

The type of finance you want will affect the sources of finance you approach. For example, if you want a short-term loan you can approach banks; if you want venture capital you might be better off approaching business contacts or the Enterprise Investment Scheme.

3

what
are you
selling?

You cannot successfully sell anything nor convince investors of the business's viability unless you are clear about exactly what your product or service is. You should be able to write a clear description of what you intend to sell. To do this you need to understand its benefits and Unique Selling Point (USP). Find your business niche. Analyse your business idea's strengths and weaknesses and opportunities for promotion. You also need to research and assess the competition. Remember to work out practical issues such as where you will store stock, where your sales premises will be and how you will arrange distribution. It is also important to decide whether you will control everything or whether you will employ other people to help. Remember that production costs might determine what you sell. You also need to decide how much and in what way development will take place and the likely costs.

Defining your business

A description of what you intend to sell is one of the most important parts of your business plan. You need to provide a clear explanation of what service or product you will be selling and what it does or how you will operate it. By setting this out in writing you will be able to see whether your idea is fully developed and ready to put into the marketplace. You may be supplying both products and services, in which case you will need to explain how you will integrate them.

Your ultimate aim is to achieve revenue from sales. To do that you need to set targets and objectives for your sales. For a new business these targets will be presented in the form of sales forecasts. You will need to set out the sales forecasts according to different types of products or services (if more than one), by volume and value (if relevant), by sales into different types of customers (local/national, male/female or other groups relevant to your business) and sales by different distribution methods (e.g. post, retail stores, house-to-house sales). More information about writing the sales forecasts is given in Chapter 8.

If you have not already done so you might need to decide whether you are providing a product or service. Although we think these are easily distinguished from each other, sometimes it can be difficult to decide which definition fits what you are selling. For example, a book is a product. If you publish the book you are selling a product; if you hunt for out-of-date books for customers you are providing a book-search service. If you publish your own books and sell them at talks you give then you are providing a product (the book) and a service (the talk). The key question you should ask is: 'What am I getting paid for?'.

Define this first to decide what your actual product or service is. Write down exactly what you are providing.

Remember that in business terms a product can be touched. In non-business terms a product might simply be something you have created but which cannot be touched, such as the performance of a play. In business terms the performance of a play would be a service, the printed copy of the play a product.

If you are intending to sell a range of products or services you need to be able to describe the different components of the range and how they relate to each other.

How will you sell?

The next thing anyone reading your business plan will want to know is where you are going to sell your product or service.

Where you intend to sell will limit the type of service or product you can offer. You will not, for example, be able to provide ice creams directly to customers from your home if you have not got the facilities or space to make the ice cream and store it.

Selling it yourself

If you have a product or service that is easy to store and you can sell directly to the public you might want to sell it yourself. You need to bear in mind that if you are doing the selling, then you will have less time for running the business. This is fine if you are, for example, an artist selling your own paintings, but not if you offer a cleaning service. In the latter case, it might be more practical to employ someone to do the cleaning while you run the office.

Employing others to sell it

If you will not have the time to run as well as create or provide your service or product you will need to employ others to do the selling for you. This puts you at one remove from your customers and brings into question all kinds of legal and practical obligations to your employees. Readers of your business plan will want to know why you have chosen one method of selling.

Selling from home

You need to explain where you will sell your product or service. Will you be selling it from home? In which case, will you be sending a product out or selling it on the premises? Will you be providing a service where customers visit your home, or one where they will contact you at home although you never meet?

Selling through others

You might employ other people to sell for you. They might work directly from their homes or your workplace or go out to customers. Or they might sell for you in a retail outlet.

Selling through space

You may decide to sell by providing your product or service by mail or on the internet. In this way you do not meet your customers, but you may have to consider things such as storage, insurance and credit card safety. However you will be selling, you need to be able to explain the method clearly.

What is your USP?

Everything you sell should have a USP – a Unique Selling Point. That is the one thing that will make your customers buy what you are selling, and buy it from *you*. It is important that you know what makes your product or service different from everyone else's. What makes it original? This doesn't mean that it has to be necessarily completely different from what other people sell, but it should offer something original in the way of benefit to the customer, otherwise why would anyone buy it in preference to others? Think carefully about how what you will sell is different.

Of course, there are many more ways in which you could provide a USP, but you must have one. If you are not sure of your USP, try asking your friends what they think makes it different.

Nobody will buy what you sell unless it has some benefit for them. This is a key point that must be included in your business plan. You may have found a USP but it may not be something that customers want. What you sell must provide one or more benefits for your customers. Your USP might be a benefit, but not necessarily. If you sell milk in orange bottles it will be different, but how does it benefit the customer? If you explain that it will make it easier to find in a large fridge, they might be tempted (but perhaps not). You need to explain what your customer will get out of what you sell. Bear in mind too that not all benefits are tangible. You will not only be selling a product or service but also aspirations. Consider whether what you sell will, for example, improve people's lifestyles, give them an advantage at work, demonstrate their financial status or show them to be part of an up-to-date trend. What you sell should make people feel good about themselves.

What is your market

It is no good having a brilliant idea but being unable to sell the result because there is no demand for it. To find out who your customers will be you will need to do some basic research. You will also need to back up this research with facts and figures. In your business plan it will be no good writing that you talked to your friends and lots of people thought it was a good idea. How many people in your area want it? Would they buy it if you provided it? How would they want to get it?

The image your product or service projects is part of what will sell it. Readers of your business plan will want to discover whether you are aware of that image and how you will ensure that it will be suitable for your customers. The image can be the result of many things such as status, utility or aspirations. For example, if what you sell will be something that makes people feel part of a select or popular group, then you are selling status. If you are selling something that everyone feels to be necessary because of its usefulness, then you are selling utility. It is no good selling something useful that customers perceive to be shameful to possess or use. Remember the jokes about a certain kind of car? The car was perfectly good but in the public's mind it had an image of being an embarrassment to drive. It took hard work and a lot of money for the company to overcome the wrong kind of image.

Part of the image your product or service will project will be determined by the niche into which you wish to fit it. For example, to sell to a particular group of people you need to ensure that the image fits with what they will find desirable. So you might wish to sell to the 13 to 18 year age group and would therefore want to project an image that would be exciting, fashionable, cheap and instantly available.

How will your business work?

If you start by making the product or providing the service yourself, you have complete control over the production process, everything from the design to the packaging. This is really only possible if you only ever intend to sell a very limited number of products or provide a service well within your personal limits of delivery. Once you intend to produce or provide more than you can deliver personally, you will need to employ other people. The decision on whether to stay small and work alone or expand and employ other people is one that successful small businesses have to make eventually.

Once you employ other people to make your product you are probably at the stage when you will need to employ other people to sell it as well. Once you do that you have the problems that come with employing others and you are once again at one or more removes from what you are selling.

What you sell is tied in with how you sell. If you want to sell a product yourself but intend to sell to a great many people then you might have to employ other people. If you want to sell to a lot of people but can only provide one daily service call then you will have to employ others or alter your expectations.

Distribution is tied to what you can sell. If you want to operate by sending a product by ordinary post you can't sell a massage service or sell very bulky products (unless you use a different kind of postal service). You will be limited to such things as books, slim boxes, small products, etc. On the other hand the product or service might dictate the method of distribution. So selling made-to-measure shoes might mean that you can only do so by personal contact with the customer. Or selling computers to foreign countries might mean that you have to do so through a third party.

What you sell might also be determined by how much it will cost you to create the product or start the service. If these costs are too high you have some alternatives:

* ask for more money in the form of loans or investments or grants
* change the product or service
* change the way you sell.

The price of what you sell is important in the scheme of things. What you sell might be determined by its possible selling price. If you want to raise a lot of money quickly then you might consider selling something that is already popular or has wide appeal. If you want to enter a niche market then you might be able to do so by selling at a higher price because of the scarcity value. (Pricing is discussed in more detail in Chapter 8.)

SWOT analysis

This concept of analysing a problem, called SWOT analysis, has many relevancies. It can help you examine what makes your product saleable and how you relate to the competition.

* **Strengths.** What are the benefits of your product or service? What benefits does the competition offer? Why and how does your product offer better or more benefits than theirs?
* **Weaknesses.** What weaknesses can you find? Does the competition have the same or different weaknesses? Can you turn the weaknesses into benefits or strengths? How can you reduce the weaknesses or eliminate them?
* **Opportunities.** Is there an obvious gap in the market? Are any of your competitors aiming to fill that gap? How can you adapt what you sell to make the most of the opportunities?
* **Threats.** Where are the threats coming from? Are they coming from competitors, the economic climate, government regulations, changing public perceptions and needs? How can you turn threats into strengths or opportunities?

It is rare that a product or service will not need developing or changing in the future. This might be to adapt to new trends and customer needs, to improve the product or service, or to comply with new regulations or delivery changes. The costs of doing this must be estimated and included in your plan.

You need to include a summary paragraph in your plan explaining the pros and cons of your product or service after you are clear about what you are offering customers and what the competition is.

4

who are your customers?

Unless you know who your customers are you cannot direct your sales effort efficiently. Customers can be organizations and corporate bodies as well as individuals. You cannot target customers effectively unless you have a lot of information about them. Use market research to discover your customers' likes and dislikes and how, when and where they want to obtain your product or service. The best way to find out what your customers want is to ask them directly through interviews, questionnaires or observation. You can use secondary sources produced by other people to add to your customer research. If necessary, divide your customers into specific groups for different types of marketing. Look at what you sell from your customers' point of view. Decide how you will deal with any complaints. Your plan needs to show that there is a market for what you sell and that the demand will be long-term.

Knowing your customers

Your customers can cover a wide range of people. Don't forget that they might include organizations as well as individuals. Unless you are dealing with individual customers you will be selling to people within an organization, large or small. Your approach will vary according to their role within the organization. What you sell must appeal to them as representatives of their organization. You also need to take into account the concerns of people who help you get your product to customers.

The product or service must not only appeal to customers but must satisfy criteria that concern these people or they will not deal with you. An example of this is the agency that will not ask its reps to sell a book because it does not satisfy criteria that will make it sell, such as a striking cover. When you are deciding what to sell you need to take all these things into account.

You cannot target your customers effectively unless you know a great deal of information about them. Anyone reading your plan needs to know that you know precisely who your customers are and where to find them. Any marketing you do will be far less effective if you are simply telling everyone that your product is available and hoping that the people who will be really interested will find it.

Customer information

You will need to use market research to find out about your customers. The aims of market research are to provide people running a business with the information they need to make informed decisions. Market research involves gathering, analysing, interpreting and presenting data in an organized way. It can then be used to help inform market decisions. You can do basic market research yourself but can also employ a market researcher or market research agency.

Information about your customers will help you target them and convince readers of your business plan that you know what you are doing. After all, you need to know who your customers are so that you can sell to them and continue to sell to them. Knowing your target customers convinces readers that your business has a viable future.

The more details you have about your customers, the better you can target your product or service to their needs and target any marketing to reach them.

Geography

Where your customers live is obviously very important. If you supply a product you might be able to sell it over a much wider area than a service, particularly if the service is geared towards particular local needs.

Age

An obvious piece of information you need about your customers is their age. Some products or services will be uniquely suitable for certain age groups, for example rattles for a baby, alcoholic drinks for over-18s, pensions for working age adults. Others might cross age barriers, for example trainer shoes, jeans, food, holidays. If what you sell is to do well then it must be targeted at the correct age range and readers will expect to see knowledge of this in your plan.

Sex

This needs careful thought. Is your product or service suitable for only men or only women? Nowadays, and bearing in mind sex discrimination laws, there will be virtually nothing that either sex might not find desirable, but there will be things that one sex might prefer to another. Although you should be happy to sell to whoever wants it (except in the case of things deemed lawfully unsuitable for anyone under-age) you might want to target one sex or another.

Education

What you sell might be more appealing to people who have a certain level or type of education. For example, you might assume (perhaps erroneously) that classical records are more likely to be bought by people who have been through higher education.

Or you might be producing an educational toy that would appeal mainly to primary school children (or their parents).

Residence

The type of property your customers are likely to live in might also have a bearing on the type of service or product you offer or to whom you direct it. This might be because it is directly related to the type of building or because customers will be buying into aspirations to create a certain type of residence (for example, town dwellers wanting to recreate the rustic look). Or you might make assumptions about the type of people who live in certain kinds of property.

When and how often customers buy

This is important to find out because it will affect how you run your business. This needs to be made explicit in your plan. What you sell might be seasonal or affected by other influences. Your customers might buy a product or service frequently because they consider it essential or it might be an occasional luxury or emergency purchase. Knowledge of your customers' buying habits is vital to ensuring that your product or service is available at the right time or in the right quantities.

Why buy it?

It is also important to find out why customers buy the product or service. Is it something that everyone in their peer group buys? Have they been affected by advertisements? Do they like the colour, shape, price? If you are going to sell to them you need to know what will attract them to what you sell.

Likes and dislikes

It might seem odd to try to discover what your customers like but it is an important part of understanding them and whether they would be receptive to what you sell. Companies frequently go to great lengths to try to discover their customers' hobbies, shopping preferences, possessions and so on because it provides a more detailed picture of their clients.

Why these customers?

For some businesses your customer base will be obvious — if you sell a coat for rabbits you will be selling to pet owners, for example. If you sell something that could appeal to a wide range of customers your customer base might not be so obvious. Think in terms of segmentation, that is positioning your product or service to particular sections of the population. If you divide your customers into groups you can tailor what you sell and how you sell it to each group. The segments need to be large enough to be profitable but measurable so that you can tell whether you have reached your target customers.

Segmentation

You might segment your customers into groups based on broad terms such as their attitudes, employment or income. Or perhaps by location, type of buyer, type of dwelling or family type. If you sell to industry you could segment by industrial sector, number of employees or country. So one business might target mothers under 30 living in south-east England who work outside the home and earn less than £15,000. Another might aim at biscuit-makers in Eastern Europe with 10 to 60 employees.

Customers as organizations

Customers can be organizations as well as individuals. Although it is the organizations themselves that you have to sell to, you will be pitching towards the individuals in organizations who have the power to buy. Your product or service must be what is required by them and they will have their own likes and dislikes.

Your first task will be to find out what the organization needs. Then find out who in the organization makes decisions about buying, who has the spending power, who decides what features a product or service needs. You need to find out what their spending limits are and how they make their purchasing decisions.

You might have to be on their list of approved suppliers and, if so, you need to find out how to get on it. Once on it, will you be automatically invited to bid? Who do you need to keep in contact with?

How to reach your customers

You need to find out how your customers prefer to receive what you sell. If they prefer to buy by mail they may be put off by a product or service that can only be obtained from a shop. Knowing this will not only help you reach your customers more effectively but also determine your distribution costs.

You need to define the area you intend to deliver to and sell in. Don't overestimate your capabilities with delivery but be prepared to expand if your business does well.

Obtaining customer information

It is all very well saying that you need to know who your customers are, but how do you find out the basic information about them? This is part of the job of market research. This is not the place to give detailed instructions on how to go about creating and carrying out a market research project; there are many good books available. However, a brief explanation of what sources you can use follows.

Interviews

The best way to find out what your potential customers want is simply to ask them. This can be done by conducting interviews with them yourself or by employing other people to do so. The interviews might be conducted one-to-one or in focus groups. Either way, you need to decide what questions you will ask by deciding what you want to know. Even if you decide that an informal discussion would be more useful, you still need to know what questions you want answers to and so be able to guide the discussion.

Questionnaires

This is a popular method of discovering customers' likes and dislikes. A carefully constructed questionnaire will contain specially chosen questions which are relevant but unbiased and which allow the recipients time to answer them. They can be handed out in the street to likely targets, posted, put on the internet, emailed or kept at a stall. If you provide a space for 'further comments' you can broaden the questionnaire's usefulness.

You should not need to ask for respondents' names and contact details. If you do need to do so, ensure that their rights under the Data Protection Act are maintained.

Response time might be slower if recipients delay sending the form back. You need to factor in costs for postage and printing.

Observation

If you sell a product you can go to the point of sale and watch what customers look at, what they buy, what they ask for. Or, if possible, go to places where they use the product and see what problems they have and how they use it. If you sell a service, accompany a service provider on some visits to customers to assess their satisfaction and see any practical problems for yourself.

Hall tests

In this research method selected people are invited to a nearby hall or large room close to a shopping centre. They are asked to evaluate products and are interviewed about them. The tests might take place in several different towns to achieve a larger sample.

Testing the market

You could try selling your product or service in a limited area for a limited time to see customers' reactions.

Secondary sources

Secondary sources are those which have been produced by other people. They might include directories, customer lists, information from market research companies, newspapers, etc. You might need to employ a market researcher to answer some of these questions. Some questions can be answered by searching the internet or using a good encyclopaedia, but for others you might need to take a more sideways look.

The customers' viewpoint

Customer satisfaction should be at the heart of your business, and your plan will need to address this. This encompasses not only ensuring that what you sell is what they want but providing it in a way that they prefer and dealing with customer complaints. You need to be able to explain in your plan how you will deal with this.

Look at what you sell from your customers' viewpoint. Are you simply providing what you *think* they want or have you analysed your research and found out what they *really* want and what they consider the important features are. You might discover, for example, that while you think they will be impressed by the colour or by the price, that they really value the after-sales service and size.

Calculating demand

You will need to justify your choice of customers, that is the segments of the market you are aiming at, by showing what the demand for your product or service will be. Your plan should include an indication of the total demand for your product or value of the market. This is done using a particular market segment (or for some businesses, your total market) over a specific period of time (often one year) in specified market conditions. To calculate this you need to multiply the number of target customers by the number of products or number of times your service is used over the course of a year by the average price per item or service. So if you estimate there are 20,000 potential customers in a particular geographical area you are targeting and they each buy six products or services each year at £45 a time then the total market value is:

Potential customers × (number of product/service per year per customer × price of product service)

For example:

20,000 × (6 × £45) = 20,000 × £270 = £540,000

You can also calculate the value as a percentage of customer spending in that sector of the market.

5

marketing strategy

Marketing is part of your overall strategy to attract and keep customers. You need to understand your market before you can market your product or service. This involves finding out about trends and influences that affect the business and analysing the competition. Research your competitors by talking to their customers and looking at their marketing. When you have done this you can decide which marketing methods to use. The internet has become an important marketing tool so you will need to have an effective web presence. You should also keep up to date with new technology so that you can compete with similar businesses. Also important in a marketing strategy is knowledge of what barriers there are to your business entering the market for customers. Select your pricing system carefully. Your business plan will contain a description of the market and the competition and your marketing strategy, including intended promotional activity.

Understanding the market

Many people think that marketing consists only of the promotional and publicity activity which is the public side of any effort to attract and keep customers. In reality, it is much more than that. It is part of an overall strategy to put the needs of the customer first.

You first need to understand what the market situation is now and what trends and influences will affect your business. The research you have done to find out who your customers are and what they want will be an important part of your marketing plan. You also need to find who your competitors are and what you can offer that they do not. Before you can explain your marketing strategy you need to show that you understand your market and will be pitching sales and promotional strategy correctly.

It is very important to have an awareness of the major trends that affect your market. These might be as self-evident as the major festival seasons, or relationship to college terms or the football season, or more irregular trends such as a new interest in technology, environmental concerns, or a change in house prices.

You can get information about market trends from the internet, business and trade magazines, government publications and so on. If the trend is relevant to your business you will need to include a chart showing the trend in your business plan.

Market conditions

The plan will need to show that you are aware of other restraints or forces affecting your business: these might be social, political, economic or governmental. For example, the political climate might not be right, there might be a downward or upward turn in the economy forecast, new laws might have been introduced for your type of business, there might be geographical limitations, and so on.

New technology

New technology in the form of increased internet competition and more competitive processes means that you need to keep up to date in this area. Any business needs an internet presence to compete effectively. You need to be aware of the technology that is used in your industry and explain how you will keep up with it.

The four Ps of marketing

Your plan should include information based on the four Ps of marketing, that is *product*, *price*, *promotion* and *place* (distribution).

* product – what you are selling
* price – how much is the selling price
* promotion – how you get customers to buy
* place – where and how you will sell.

Analysing the competition

Find out in more detail who your competitors are and how your product or service will compare with them. If you fail to include an analysis of the competition in your business plan, potential backers will not take it seriously. You need to explain how your business has or will obtain a competitive advantage in the market.

It is important to explain in business plan how you will stop your competitors poaching your customers. Any potential investors or lenders will need to be reassured that you have a strategy in place for keeping your share of the market and indeed growing within it. You also need to explain the *barriers to entry*. These are areas where your competitors might have the advantage and you will have to explain in your plan how you will deal with them.

Researching your competitors is done in a similar way to the market research methods about customers. Knowledge of your competitors is vital to see how their business offerings and methods compare with yours. You also need to do some basic research to discover where people normally buy your product and service and who from. You also need to find out what they like and dislike about any rival's offerings and what they would ideally like to see from yours.

A good way of finding out what customers think of your competitors is simply to ask them. Go to places where your competitors' products or services are being offered and talk to people who have used them or are about to use them.

There is nothing to stop you obtaining any literature that your competitors produce so that you can gauge their strengths and weaknesses. This might include brochures, advertising and company reports. You can also look in the trade or business magazines to see whether there are any articles about the companies.

If you want a professional report on your competitors then you need to employ a market researcher or market research company. You can find these through the market research organizations.

Your market share

You need to show that you understand realistically how much of the market share your product or service will expect to gain initially and over a period of time. You can gauge this by reading company reports and looking at the company websites on the internet.

Pricing policy

The amount of market share you have estimated as well as your potential customers will dictate the price you will charge. You need to balance the price with quality. Will you be cutting quality to sell the product or service cheaper and undercut competitors, or will you be pricing it for a more discerning market and relying on quality to attract customers? Will you be pricing it at a similar level to your competitors and offering something unique? If you will be undercutting your competitors you will have to show how you will make a profit, and if you will be charging more you will need to demonstrate the unique selling point (USP) that will encourage customers to favour you over your competitors.

In your plan you need to include a section explaining your pricing system and how it relates to the prices your competitors charge. You need to justify the price and explain what you would do if competitors changed their prices.

Product life

You will need to explain how your product or service will go on being saleable after the launch. Therefore you need to work out the product's life.

Brand image

To sell effectively you need to create a brand or image that customers will associate with what you sell. This can be used in promotional activities. Sometimes it is put into more tangible form. Examples are a company logo or a recognizable advertising theme.

Promoting your product or service

Once you have decided what your product or service will be, you need to find ways of getting it noticed by the general public and keeping it in the public's mind. Unless people know what you are offering they cannot buy it. Once your product or service is being sold you need to keep it in front of the public's eye so that they return to it again and again. You also need to have a clear timescale in mind for each marketing activity.

There are a number of ways of promoting a product or service. Not all of them will be suitable or affordable for your business, but you should explain in your business plan which you will be using for promotional purposes and why they will be effective.

Advertising

Many people confuse advertising and publicity. But although they seem similar they are different. Advertising is paid for by the client whereas publicity is free. Advertising can be done in any part of the media but not all will be appropriate for you. If you are a small business or just starting out using the small ads, trying to get good publicity may be more effective and cheaper than paying for advertising.

If you are a franchisee then the franchisor will provide advertising and promotional material that is acceptable to the franchise as a whole. If you want to use your own promotional material or arrange advertising yourself you will need to get it approved by the franchisor. This is so that the franchise maintains its overall image.

You must be able to justify any claims that you make in advertising under the Trades Description Act and Advertising Standards Authority Code of Practice. You can get advice about this from your local Trading Standards Office.

Publicity

Publicity is achieved through unpaid mention or recommendation by others. Because no money changes hands it is perceived by the public (sometimes erroneously) to be unbiased and therefore a more reliable judgement on a business. There are several ways of gaining publicity for a business. Most of them involve some basic costs such as postage or phone calls and these must be included in your marketing budget.

Press releases

The basis of free publicity is the press release. This provides news about your product or business or its personnel to the media, and if a journalist considers it interesting enough, a story will be created from it. You may even get a photograph in the press. Publicity is generally considered better than advertising because it is deemed more objective and therefore more trustworthy.

Articles

Articles are another way of getting your business noticed by the media. If you can write a straightforward piece about a new aspect of your business you may be able to place it in the press. Call up editors and offer a piece but don't expect to get paid. Keep to any guidelines about length and deadlines. Where possible include add-ons such as a brief biography or boxes containing further information. Don't forget small presses, for example newsletters, club magazines, university/school magazines, etc.

Publicity events

These can be anything that might engender publicity in the media, such as demonstrations, exhibitions, events for journalists and sponsored sports. For example, taking your product or service to halls, rooms, meetings, etc., and demonstrating it to the public can be a very effective way of promoting your product or service.

Leaflets/catalogues

Simple leaflets can be created either on your computer or by professionals and these can be used for direct mailing or handed out for example at lectures or demonstrations. If you have more than one product or different aspects of your service to sell, you may need a catalogue. This can be a simple photocopied booklet or a full-colour production.

Direct mailing

Direct mailing is a recognized and well-used way of looking for customers. You can buy a mailing list from agencies or create your own. There are mailing list agencies that will send your promotional material to your list for you. You and the agency must comply with the Data Protection Act. Direct mail needs to be targeted; it is a waste of time sending a mailing to everyone.

Internet

You can use the internet for marketing in two ways. First, you can create your own web-page (or get someone to design one for you). Remember to put in your contact details and if necessary arrange online buying. Offset costs by links to other sites. Second, you can use email to contact your customers with their permission. This is cheap and quick but remember spam (unsolicited mail), is illegal.

Special offers, free gifts

By encouraging your customers to try your product or service by using special promotions you hope to entice them to become regular customers. You might want to hand out free gifts – for example, pens, mugs, mouse mats – or sell two for one for a week.

Personal recommendation

Word of mouth is one of the most effective of marketing tools, though difficult for a business to generate. Easier to obtain are written testimonials or endorsements from individuals and companies who either use or would like to use your product or service. Get their permission to use their endorsements in your marketing activities.

Salespeople

If you use salespeople they can promote your business wherever they go. They can do so in retail outlets, door-to-door or as sales reps, whichever is relevant. They can answer questions and provide you with immediate feedback.

Monitoring and resources

It is common mistake, particularly in smaller businesses, to be overwhelmed by an unexpectedly high response to a marketing campaign. Before you start you will need to have strategies in place for responding to any unexpected demand or complaints from the public. This should be included in your business plan.

You should be clear about what personnel you need to implement your marketing strategy. Will you do it all yourself, enlist your family and friends, employ a marketing manager and staff? Much will depend on the size of your business and your financial expectations. However, do not make the mistake of assuming that marketing is an unimportant part of a business.

Even the most cost-effective of promotion and publicity campaigns will cost money. This will not only include the actual tools you use but also things such as time, travel, printing and employing others for the campaign. You will need to provide a breakdown of marketing costs both for the initial launch and for ongoing use.

Whatever promotional activities you decide to pursue you need to ensure that you do not fall foul of the law or mislead the public. There are certain things you must do. You must comply with the Data Protection Act. If you keep a mailing list for direct mail advertising, for example, you may well have to pay a fee to the Data Protection Agency as well as comply with rules about removing people from the list and gaining permission for their inclusion. There are also laws governing advertising, both its contents and its use.

6

managing your business

The management of your business and the number and type of staff you employ will be an important part of your business plan. You will need to provide details of all your managers, including their CVs, references and qualifications. Don't forget to include details of your own expertise. Be clear about what skills your employees will need to operate the business effectively. The type and number of other staff you employ will depend on the type and size of your business, but this information should be included together with information about training, appraisal and monitoring of their performance. You must be prepared to treat your employees well and motivate them. If you need to use outside experts this should be made clear. Remember to find out how to comply with legal aspects of employment. You also need to work out what standards of service you will expect from your staff.

Personnel

The way your business is managed will affect its efficiency, the type and number of staff, staff costs and the type of product or service you can offer.

First and foremost any investor will want to know whether your business has the skills to deliver the plan. Those skills will be provided by you and any partners or employees, so you must ensure that you can convince investors that the necessary skills will be available.

Management

Who will be managing your business? This is a basic question that you need to answer. You might be running it on your own, in which case you will need to explain how you will manage not only providing the product or service yourself, but how you will deal with the administrative tasks (all that paperwork and all those phone calls) by yourself.

Remember that if you are part of a management team, you need to include your own details in the business plan. If you are watching the business from the sidelines you will still need to inform readers who you are and why you are presenting the plan. If you are in charge of the business then you will need to have an overview of the business and readers will expect to see that reflected in the plan.

In the plan you should not only describe your skills and expertise but explain how you will be leading the company, if that will be your role. The success of a business depends very much on the personality of the person at the top and how that is communicated through management to staff. How do you see yourself acting in the role of leader or a partner? You will need to show that you have an understanding of the business as a whole and that you have an excellent understanding of the business.

If you will be managing the business on your own it might be hard to convince people in a position to help that you alone have all skills and experience to run your business without other managers. This is particularly difficult if you do not have the relevant experience but are convinced that you can make the business a success. In your plan you will need to demonstrate to readers that you have other equivalent experience. You should include references from people who can confirm that you have skills or qualifications that are equally useful and relevant. It is worth including these, even if they do not relate exactly to the business.

If you will have partners or intend to employ managers you need to be able to stress the skills they will bring to the company. Ideally, have key managers identified so that you can stress their skills and include their CVs and references in the plan. You should explain exactly who will do what and explain how individuals will resolve any weaknesses in your management structure.

Staff

Although your business plan will concentrate on the key managers for your business, you need to decide what other staff you need and how many.

You might start with a certain number of employees but expect to increase the number as your business expands. At each stage you need to be able to say how many staff you need for each kind of job and why you need that number then.

Consider the costs of the number of staff you have in mind. Do you need them all? Or would it be more cost-effective to outsource to others? For example, you might be able to eliminate salespeople if you use specialist agencies, wholesalers or distributors. Look at how the competition deals with staffing. Can you do something similar?

You must be clear about the skills your business needs in its staff. These might be practical, such as IT skills, van drivers, craft skills, or specific qualifications such as accountancy, personnel management, law, etc. As well as these skills you will need people with such things as managerial skills and promotional skills.

You need to ensure that all the skills you need are available in the managers you employ and your staff.

General skills

The specific skills you will need for your business will depend on the type of business and the specific jobs within it, but most of the above skills will be necessary. Not all your employees will have all the skills, but there may well be some basic skills that you expect all your employees (and yourself) to have.

It is important to show in your plan that you know what skills your business will need in the future. So, apart from demonstrating that the business can start with the necessary skills, you must work out what additional skills the business might need later. You must then explain how you will get staff with those skills – will you recruit them? Train existing staff? Employ outside experts for the short term when necessary? All this you must decide and cost for your plan.

External help

If you might need to involve outside help from time to time, this must be explained and accounted for and costed in the business plan. For example, occasionally you might need to employ a public relations firm, market research company, solicitor, sales reps, PR expert, accountant or patent preparer.

Qualifications

Once you know what skills you need, decide what level of qualification you will need from applicants. Will you need college certificates/diplomas/degrees, several years of expertise, professional or trade qualifications, or will you create a test for applicants to pass?

Staff costs

In any business plan the costs must be spelt out clearly. Once you have decided on the number and skills of your personnel you need to work out exactly how much you will be paying them. Remember that you need to take into account not only salaries and wages but such things as National Insurance, holiday pay, sickness pay, etc.

Recruitment

How will you recruit your staff? Will you put ads in the local papers, advertise in professional magazines, put out radio ads nationwide, rely on word of mouth, employ your friends? This will take time and money and however you do it, it needs to be justified in your plan.

Type of employee

What kind of employee are you looking for? Are you looking for people with training or who are willing to learn your ways? People who work well as a team or who can work well on their own? People who are creative and energetic or reliable and efficient (possibly, but not necessarily, both)? Unless you are clear about the kind of person you want working with you, you will not get a team together that works well together.

How you treat your staff

The success of your business will depend on how you treat your staff. This is not only how you all get on together at work but how you involve them in the business. It also includes a lot of things that are laid down by law. In your business plan you need to show that you have thought about the structure and practical side of employing staff. Once you have explained how many staff you need, with what skills, and how much they will cost, you need to explain how they will work together and how you will keep them. You might be running a business where staff stay only a short time (for example, fast food, restaurants) or one where staff stay for several years or more (for example, the professions). This needs to be taken into consideration when explaining how your business will be managed.

Managers need to be motivated so that they can motivate their staff in turn. Be supportive both of your managers and your staff. The success of your business lies largely on their shoulders. How will you motivate your managers and what will it cost?

If you intend to provide any of these incentives for your managers or staff you will need to include the costs in your financial statements.

Training

If your managers or staff do not have all the relevant skills your business needs you will need to decide how you will deal with training. Will you train staff on the job? Arrange day-release courses? Provide a course of training immediately on joining the business? Any training needs to be costed and included in your financial statements.

Other considerations

Even if you work by yourself there are legal aspects to be considered. At the least you need to understand what you need to do regarding National Insurance, VAT (if relevant) and income tax. If you employ other people then there are more aspects to be taken into account. If you are not sure of any of these you need to take advice from an accountant or solicitor.

Every part of your business might be subject to legal or financial restraints. You need to know what these are for your business and how they will affect it. It is no good claiming that you didn't comply with a law because you didn't know about it. Any one reading your plan will expect you to understand what the law requires of your business and how you are going to deal with it. So you might need to employ outside advisers to ensure that you understand the law and how it relates to your business and that you are able to include how you are going to comply with the law in your plan correctly.

For your plan you should estimate the number of staff you will employ and check with an accountant for advice about how much insurance, tax and so on will cost you per staff member. This needs to be included in your accounts.

If you will be in a business that has a trade body or professional organization, then you need to join it and to get advice from it about any laws that you need to comply with. For some businesses – for example, solicitors, architects – membership of the relevant professional organization is mandatory before you can start trading.

In your plan you need to show not only how your business will be managed but also what standards you expect from your staff (including yourself and any partners). It is the people in a business who create the standards that customers see. A shoddy service or product will lose you customers and the reputation of the business will suffer. The plan should demonstrate that you understand the need for standards and explain what they are and how you will attain and keep them. A successful business is one that has high standards and maintains them.

In your plan you therefore need a statement about what your standards are, how you will train your staff to ensure that they meet those standards, and how you will monitor their performance.

If you are running a franchise, the way you manage your business will be largely determined by the franchise owner. You need to be clear about what help you can expect to get from them and whether that help will be ongoing or only during the start-up period. There might also be limitations on the amount or type of financial and other benefits that you can offer your staff. For example, their salaries, holidays and benefits may be determined by the franchise owner as part of the franchise agreement. If you are going to run a franchise you should include copies of the franchise agreement, operating rules and any other documents or manuals that the franchisor provides. As the franchisor will have had much experience of helping franchisees, you would do well to ask their help in preparing your business plan.

Managing your business does not just involve knowing what your staff will be doing and dealing with the legal aspects. There are a lot of practical things that you will need to explain in your plan. You will need to decide, for example, what record-keeping system you will use and whether all your records will be computerized and if so which system to use and who will be in charge of keeping it up to date. Will you have standards for producing letters and documents and which IT packages will you use? How will you process your orders? Will your employees belong to a trade union?

Readers of your plan will want to know not just who will be managing your business but how staff will be appraised and performance monitored. They will need to know that you have considered how to ensure that standards are maintained and that key staff are given opportunities for training and career advancement. The skills your business needs might change over time and you need to ensure that your managers and staff keep up with the needs of the business as far as skills are concerned.

Work out how often monitoring will be done and how it will be recorded. Remember that monitoring needs to be acted on. If standards or ways of working are not successful, you need to decide how they will be changed and what support your staff will need.

7

operating the business

Efficient operation of your business is a key component of success. In your business plan you need to explain where your business will be located, what machinery or plant you have or need to obtain, who your suppliers will be, what storage facilities you need, how the production process works, how delivery will be arranged, what hours you will operate and how the product or service will be made available to the customer. This should be described in your plan to show that you know how the business will operate on a day-to-day basis. All parts of your business should adhere to good business practices. If you will be working from home you still need to describe the practicalities of running your business and comply with any legalities. If using other premises for any business purpose you need to take into account costs of the building and transportation.

You probably know a great deal about your business, but might find it hard to put it into words. You need to be able to do this so that any potential investors will be reassured that you have a detailed understanding of how your business will work in day-to-day terms.

Keeping up with technology

Before you look in detail at the rest of your business operation, decide from the outset how much you will use information technology (IT). Nowadays, it's a vital part of any business and you will not be competitive unless you make the best use of it. The type of IT equipment you invest in will dictate how efficient your business is and how effective your communications are. You need to decide this at the outset so that you can include the costs in your business plan. You also need to decide whether you intend to invest in other IT equipment later and how often you will need to replace it.

In your business plan you should explain how your business will be improved by using IT and how it will make it competitive. If you can, see what IT your competitors use. For example, if they all have websites then you must have one or lose your customers to competitors with a web presence.

Business administration

The administration of your business is a prime concern. All parts of your business will need to be subject to good administration practices such as invoicing, stock-taking, order processing, secretarial work, receiving stock, sales recording, accounting, warehouse processes, and so on. You need to convince readers of your plan that you know how your business will operate on a day-to-day basis. It is the administration of the business that will ensure that all parts of your business will operate efficiently. You need to decide who is going to deal with which part of the administrative process and what costs will be involved. You might be able to combine these jobs or equipment. But you need to work this out beforehand so that you can include the costs in your plan.

You need to work out how administration needs link with other areas of the business and what training staff need. You also need to decide how to install and evaluate administration methods.

Premises and location

You need to consider not only where the business offices are but where any product is made or service provided. You might operate a small business entirely from your home, but if you are selling something you might need a shop. If you are providing a service you might need premises to do it from, for example running a yoga class would mean leasing a hall. A larger business might require separate office space, a factory or a large showroom. You also need to explain how the location of your business relates to any competition.

Much will depend on the nature of your business, of course, but to save costs as your business gets under way you might be able to use space you already have for a temporary period. However, there are alternatives to the standard business premises. By thinking laterally and asking around you might find that you could, for example, rent a room from a friend, share a work space with others, rent a meeting room in a hotel, etc.

Premises

At its most basic the location of your business could be your own home. In that case you need to explain where that is, what area of your home will be used for the business, how you will deal with integrating work into home life, and whether you have understood and complied with any insurance, mortgage, safety requirements that might apply. Your local authority might need to be consulted if there will be a lot of vehicles or people coming to your home; you may be subject to inspections if you intend to sell food cooked in your own kitchen.

For larger scale businesses or those that need separate production or retail premises you have a greater set of problems. You will need to locate premises and arrange to buy or lease them. You might need planning permission to built, extend or adapt them.

You need to justify the site in relation to access to your customers and means of production. You need to ensure that your business will not disturb neighbours or cause environmental problems.

There are more technical problems to be dealt with by using a separate site. Far more regulatory controls come into play. Before your business starts you need to get details of these and find out how you need to comply with them. Details of any certificates you receive and consents must be included in your business plan.

You might have enough space to work in at home. But there are other places where you can operate your business. If your business is small you might be able to use a garage or rent space under the railway arches. You can rent office space or perhaps use a purpose-built shed in the garden. Larger businesses might need a factory, warehouse, large offices and retail outlets.

Location

Decide where you want the business to be located. If you are supplying goods or services that don't need you to meet customers your home might be fine. Otherwise you need to decide whether it will be located close to where your customers will be, or close to a prospective workforce, and in what relationships to your competitors.

You need to include the costs of buildings in your business plan. This will include not only the cost of buying or leasing the premises, if relevant, but ongoing costs such as lighting or heating. You will also need to include the costs of getting the premises into a fit state for your business. You might need to pay for altering the internal layout, building additions or repairs, redecoration, soundproofing, improving access, improving lighting and heating or providing toilets. You must also consider the needs of any customers or employees who might have disabilities now or in the future and so your premises might need to be adapted for disabled access.

Storage

Before you decide where to work, evaluate how much storage space you need. If you only need to store printer paper and toner and a few books then working from home will cause few problems for storage. If you need to store hundreds of items of raw materials for your product or boxes of the finished product, or need a lot of equipment for your service, then you will need larger storage space. This might be part of your production premises or your storage might be separate. You should work out exactly what storage space you need now and allow for increased production in the future. If you store materials or finished products away from the production process you need to take into account the cost of transporting these to and from the various sites.

Storage is subject to its own conditions. You need to pay particular attention to fire safety, insurance, and any laws governing the storage of vulnerable products such as foodstuffs or inflammable goods. Work out where your storage will be and how much it will cost to buy or lease space.

Plant and equipment

Even the most basic of home businesses will need some equipment – a phone and a computer as well as any machines and tools necessary for the business. Larger businesses might require heavy machinery or plant.

Your plan will need to include details of exactly what equipment or plant your business needs to operate and details of how much they will cost to buy or lease. You need to assess how much they will lose value over the years of the plan and estimate how much they will cost to replace. You will also need to supply details of the running costs of the equipment and an estimate of the costs of any peripherals that will need replacing regularly, for example, printing ink and paper for a printer, parts for machinery, etc.

If you will be using vehicles you need to take into account their cost to buy or rent, the cost of tax and insurance, petrol, replacement parts, and so on.

Using your own car to transport products or visit clients is a possibility. If you need to buy or hire other vehicles the cost of these and their running costs must be included in your plan.

It is tempting to assume that you need to buy all your equipment, plant, buildings, vehicles, and so on, but it may well be more cost-effective to hire or lease such things. Even quite small items can be hired from specialist concerns. Sit down and work out the comparative costs of buying and leasing.

Supply and distribution

An important part of your business operation will be getting the product or service to your customers. This has two parts: first, who will supply the product or service, and second, who will distribute it and how. If you intend to operate entirely on your own you still need to work out how to reach your customers.

Supply covers providing the product or service. If you are doing this yourself then you are the supplier. If you are buying raw materials, parts or completed products from other people, or are buying in services to sell on to your customers, then you are dealing with suppliers who can dictate the cost of these, and this can cause problems.

Set out in your plan your contingency plans for any times that your supplier lets you down. How will you get supplies or personnel in an emergency? Have you made contact with other suppliers who could accommodate you at short notice? Have you a compensation scheme prepared for customers who are let down by your service?

Your product or service has to get from your business to your customers and so distribution plays a very important part in your business operations. Unless you intend to handle the distribution yourself you need to rely on others to do so. The costs of this will be included in your plan. The problems of distribution are similar to that of supply. You need to find people who are reliable to do the job and choose the most efficient method of distribution you can afford.

Closely associated with distribution is what levels of stock you need to maintain to provide a competitive service level in the market. It is this stock level that you need to be able to maintain by your production method and for which you will need to provide adequate storage where it can be easily distributed to customers. This might be on or off any retail site.

Developing operations

Research and development is an ongoing process that is an integral part of your operations. You should be constantly striving to find new and better ways of creating, marketing and delivering your product or service. This applies as much to a small business as a large one. Any costs in terms of staff, plant, materials and so on should be included in your financial documents.

Whether simple or complex, your production methods need to be as efficient and cost-effective as possible. Nowadays, you cannot afford out-of-date or inefficient production methods unless they are an intrinsic part of the final product or service, for example, hand-made shoes or an Indian head massage. You need to calculate when would be the earliest time to update machinery and how frequently you need to retrain staff in new methods.

Compare the processes and products of your business with the industry best and see whether you compare favourably. You should aim to improve on the industry average. Benchmarking gives you something to test your business against and should be an ongoing process.

8

explaining the finances

Financial statements must be included in your business plan and are vital to the success of your presentation. These statements will indicate to potential lenders or investors the financial viability of your business and your prospects of long-term success. You will need to set up a reliable accounting system even if you will be getting an accountant to deal with the annual accounts for tax purposes. You must be honest and accurate in all financial matters. The basic documents you should include are a cash flow forecast, balance sheet and profit and loss forecast. Banks and accountants can help you prepare financial statements. There are also software packages to make the process easier. You should provide enough detail to support your forecasts. Be honest about any potential risks and try to foresee any questions you might be asked about your business finances. Normally, the detailed financial statements go in appendices.

Producing financial statements

To run a business you need at least a basic understanding of accounts. You need to produce the financial statements yourself, if possible. There are many places, including banks, from which you can get business plan templates (including the financial sections) to complete yourself. You can also buy software packages that will enable you to produce a financial statement. A good accountant is worth paying for because they will save you time and money and produce accounts that you can be confident will fulfil any regulatory requirements. However, using an accountant does not take all the responsibility from you. You must make sure that you understand the accounts and can answer questions about them.

To draw up your financial statements you will need to record things clearly. This can strike fear into many people, but it is really quite simple. Instead of putting the income and expenditure in one column, put them in two. One column will show what comes into the business and the other column will show what goes out.

The financial statements that go into your business plan are not the end of your accounting commitments. Whether you have an existing business or are starting one, you need to have an accounting system in place. A good accounting system is necessary so that you know exactly where the money goes and have the figures available for any VAT queries. You can identify debtors and spot employee malpractice.

The financial section of your business plan is where you explain how and why your business will be financially successful. You need to be able to explain how much money you need (or will need) and where you will get it from. Your financial requirements should be set out in a financial needs statement. You need to explain your present and expected financial position and future needs.

Before you start to complete any financial statement you need to research the basic financial situation of your business. Your financial statements will be a good indication of how your business will operate financially. But it is only that – an indication. Therefore, the better the research you do to underpin the statements, the more accurate they will be.

To back up your statement about how much money you need and where it will be spent you need to provide evidence. This can be done by producing a cash flow forecast and a profit and loss forecast as well as a balance sheet. Some figures you will have already; others you will have to estimate. It is important not to over or underestimate the figures.

It should go without saying that you should be honest and accurate when compiling your financial statements. Do not exaggerate forecasts or omit figures that you think might not be well received. Your readers need to know exactly where the business stands financially.

Types of financial statement

Cash flow forecast

Any potential investors or lenders will need to know whether your business is likely to survive on a monthly basis. The cash flow forecast tells you where your business will go financially over the next 12-month period. It is based on estimates backed by research for a new business. The cash flow forecast shows how your business will operate financially over time and therefore whether you will be able to pay creditors. It should provide enough information to indicate how the business will survive.

Your net cash flow equals your total monthly receipts minus your total monthly payments. To get the bank balance you add or subtract the final amount from the opening balance. It is standard practice to put minus amounts in brackets.

Balance sheet

This provides a snapshot of your business. It shows what the value of your business is now if you are already trading. If you will be starting a new business then you will have to estimate the figures to show what your business will be like under certain conditions in the future. Generally a balance sheet is calculated for the end of a financial year. It provides an overall view of your financial situation and business at a specific time, usually at the end of a year. It shows what your business's debts are and what your business is owed. It is a complete picture of your business's assets and liabilities.

Profit and loss forecast

This simply means a forecast of whether your business will make a profit or loss for a specific period. Your figures should show the results monthly for at least one year and quarterly for two more. Further ahead than that and the forecast becomes too inaccurate to be useful. Also, you would expect to reassess your calculations in the light of actual business experience after about three years. It is important to recognize that cash and profit are not the same thing in business terms. Most banks or financial institutions can provide profit and loss forms for you to complete.

Sales forecasting

To produce a cash flow forecast you need to be able to estimate what your future sales will be. You also need to be able to explain how you reached the figures you include in the forecast. You can do this by straightforward mathematical means. You can either use a forecast based on annual sales or a Moving Annual Total (MAT) method that uses the previous year's monthly sales figures to project sales. Because you need to take variables such as product, marketing and seasonal changes and other possible external changes into account, this is best calculated in a business software program. You can start by recording or estimating a year's monthly sales figures.

Be careful to record sales made on credit in the month in which the business will actually receive the cash. You will need to estimate the percentage of sales made by cash and credit. If you give credit lasting different lengths of time (for example, 30 or 60 days) make sure you estimate the percentages of credit sales for each period. In the same way, record the amounts payable according to when your suppliers demand payment, which might be different for different suppliers. Only record the due figure in the month for which you actually pay it. You might find that you run at a loss until your business gets established.

Balance sheet

What you include in your balance sheet will depend on what kind of business you have or intend to have. There are different ways to present a balance sheet. The balance sheet uses double-entry bookkeeping. The date on the sheet should be the date it was prepared and it should be prepared at the close of business on that day. If you are starting a new business the balance sheet will show an estimated forecast.

The balance sheet should be divided into two parts. The assets and liabilities must be equal, that is they must be 'balanced'.

List assets in order of:
* current assets
* long-term investments, e.g. stocks
* plant and equipment – with depreciation, if relevant
* intangible assets, e.g. patent, trademark
* other assets.

Then total your assets.

List liabilities in order of:
* current liabilities – due within 12 months
* long-term liabilities – due beyond 12 months
* other liabilities.

Then total your liabilities.

Record your owners' liabilities (net worth) and then subtract your total liabilities from your total assets.

Profit and loss statement

Depreciation applies to plant and equipment that you own and must be calculated for and included in your profit and loss forecast. There are various methods of calculating depreciation and you should take advice from an accountant about which method you should use.

You should enter the figures exclusive of VAT. Also in this statement you should record income from sales in the month when the sales are made, not when the money is received.

When forecasting sales, allow for a steady build-up during the initial period as well as any seasonal or other influences. If the business is already operating, include all completed work invoiced even if it has not been paid for yet.

Gross profit margin

This is your budgeted gross profit (total sales minus total direct costs) divided by total sales and multiplied by 100. It is represented as a percentage.

$$\text{gross profit margin (\%)} = \frac{\text{gross profit}}{\text{sales}} \times 100$$

Things to note

When preparing your profit and loss statement you need to match periods for income and costs. These should both appear in the period to which they relate to, not the period in which they occur.

When estimating depreciation write off the same amount each year based on the period for which the plant, machinery or equipment is likely to last.

Realistic forecasts

You need to make sure that you do not overestimate the likely returns your business will make. Any investor or lender will want to see a profitable and sustainable return on their money and your forecasts should show that your business will provide this. But be realistic. It is easy to fall into the trap of making false assumptions.

As mentioned at the start of this chapter, you need to provide evidence to support your forecasts. You do not need to go into details in the body of your plan although you should provide references when relevant. In the appendices you should provide notes about how you reached your forecast figures and assumptions, backing them up with research you have done. Include price lists to support your sales forecasts and guaranteed orders when available. Readers will also want to know what you will do if your financial situation does not work out as planned.

In the body of the plan you will put summaries of what your financial documents tell you. In the appendices you will put the financial details themselves. Not all the detailed information will go in the body of your plan. Put your forecast figures next to the figures that show your trading history (if relevant).

deciding
the
timetable

The business plan itself should contain information about your short-, medium- and long-term objectives. The plan should cover between three and five years of operation. When preparing your business plan there are three timescales to consider – what period your plan should cover, how long it will take to prepare the plan, and how long it will take to implement it. These will depend on the size and complexity of your business. The plan can be prepared in several stages: noting what you know, deciding what to research, doing research, writing drafts, and producing the final version. Preparations should be broken down into smaller stages. Prepare a timetable for producing your plan. Use checklists to help you organize your research and complete your plan. Allow time for obtaining any outside help with the plan that you need. You can take steps to implement the plan before you have confirmation of its acceptance.

Timetable for business forecasts

You need to be clear about your objectives. All businesses should look ahead in the short, medium and long term. Your plan should demonstrate that you know where your business will be going in the future and that you are prepared for changes and have thought about how it will be operating both practically and financially for several years ahead.

Getting the forecast period right can be tricky. You shouldn't present forecasts, either financial or setting-up, that are too brief and therefore do not take into account likely changes in your business. Nor do you want to project forecasts so far ahead that the timing and figures become meaningless and the numbers you have calculated have changed so much that you are simply guessing.

Any business plan that includes forecasts for less than a year is simply not going to convince readers. You need to persuade them that your business will last at least that long and that you have a clear idea about how it will progress both financially and operationally during that time. On the other hand, you do not need to go into minute day-to-day detail. So what is a reasonable time scale to use for your plan?

For most business you will need to provide forecasts for not only the first year but for several years after that. The first year's forecast will be detailed but the later years can be outlines. How many subsequent years will depend on the size of your business. For small businesses it will be appropriate to provide forecasts for two years subsequent to the first (three years in all); larger businesses might provide four outline years of forecasts (five years in all). Any forecasts that try to look ahead further than five years are probably in the realms of fantasy. Business life changes so rapidly nowadays that it is difficult to predict anything beyond a few years ahead with any certainty.

How long for your business?

You might have difficulty in deciding whether you need a three- or five-year plan. Think about the size of your business and how long it will take to set up. If it is a small business and will be quick to set up, then provide a three-year plan. If you want a large business or it will take some time before the business is running at full strength, then provide a five-year plan. You also need to take your staff into account. If there is only you or one or two partners, then you might be able to provide a longer-term plan than if your business will have lots of staff who change frequently and on whose commitment you cannot always rely.

Timetable for plan preparation

The only sure thing about deciding how long you need to prepare your business plan is that it will take longer than you think. Keep yourself on track by drawing up a timetable for completion of your business plan. Break down your tasks into smaller steps – for example, desk research on competitors, writing paragraphs on operations, contacting trade organizations. When you make a timetable don't put it in a drawer and forget it. You need to look at it frequently while you are gathering the information and writing the plan so that you keep on track. Make sure that you do everything that is required of you to complete the plan, particularly if you are using a form provided by the financial or other organization you are targeting. Unless you are certain that a section is unnecessary, complete it.

Don't just plunge into creating your timetable. Make sure that you understand what you need before you start. Read any documentation you are to complete so that you are clear what is required of you. If in any doubt, contact the organization you are targeting, whether a bank, investment house or other, and *ask*. Don't guess. You need to know exactly what is needed.

Also, if you intend to use outside help to create or write up your plan, make sure that you have booked them well in advance. They will need adequate time to do their work.

It will help you to plan your time if you break down what you need to do into smaller steps. You will need to check back on these if you do any new research, and double-check any figures.

One approach is to divide the timetable for creating the plan into broad sections and then break these down into more detailed stages.

Using checklists

Use checklists to help you keep on track. List all the people, information, organizations and so on that you need to deal with. Next to each item on the list write down *how* you are going to get the information. Set a target date for talking to, meeting or contacting people you need to get information from and for obtaining information for other sources. When you have got the information write the completion date beside the item. This will quickly tell you whether you are running slowly and, if so, by roughly how much and you can then adjust your timetable accordingly. When all the information is assembled you can complete the writing-up of your plan (this is covered in more detail in the following chapter).

Timetable for starting the business

It is possible to set up small businesses very quickly, especially if you will be operating on your own and already have the expertise required. Generally, you will need time to get things set up if you are starting from scratch. If you are setting up a business as part of a franchise you will get help from the franchisers and they will be able to provide guidance on any problems you are experiencing and the timescale you need to allow.

Obtaining the finance

How long this will take will depend on the type of finance you need and who will be providing it. You need to allow time for a decision to be made and for the lender, investor or grant provider to arrange for the money to reach you. They should be able to give you an idea of how long it will take them to reach a decision.

Sorting out legalities

Once you have the financial situation settled you can sort out any legalities. These might be licensing, health and safety and fire certificates, and so on. The regulatory bodies will be able to give you some idea of how long it will take to inspect and certificate (always longer than you think or would like). If you are hoping to renovate or buy premises and planning permission or other permissions for building (building regulations or listed building consent) will be required, then you must allow much longer. The council will tell you how long the process should take. You then need to allow time for the work to be done before you can move your offices or production process into the building. If this is going to take longer than you would like, you should be thinking about temporary accommodation for your business while permissions are obtained and work is going on.

Obtaining premises

You might have premises in mind but have not already obtained them. The time to do so is when you have the finances confirmed. As well as your preferred premises, you should also think of several alternatives. The usual time for buying once a sale is agreed is six weeks, although it can sometimes be done more quickly. If you are waiting in a buying chain then you cannot accurately predict the time it will take. Renting premises will be quicker assuming suitable premises are available, and this might be a sensible option as it will give you time to buy premises. If you are working from home you can use the time waiting for confirmation of your financial status to check whether there are any mortgage or council regulations you need to comply with. If there are and you cannot satisfy these, you will have to look for alternative premises.

Obtaining plant/machinery/equipment

While you are waiting for a decision about financial aid you should be searching for suppliers of necessary plant and machinery or any other equipment you need. Check out the firms' prices and their guarantees and whether they repair on your premises. Find out whether hiring would be more cost effective. If your business will be small and the equipment common, you might be able to borrow it from friends or relatives for a short period until you can afford buy or lease your own.

Hiring and training staff

If you are going to employ other people you need to sort out how to deal with their National Insurance, tax, contracts of employment and other necessary details. Contact the tax office for advice while you are waiting for the financial aspects of your business to be completed.

If your employees will need training before they can start work you need to find out how much this will cost and where it can be done, if you are not training them on the job. Preferably use training schemes that end with a recognized qualification or skill certification. This reassures you that your staff are qualified to a certain standard and enables them to build on their skills at a later date.

Producing and delivering the product or service

It will take time to produce your first batch of products or set up a service so that it can be delivered to customers. This will involve not only manufacturing or organizing what you will be selling, but arranging supply, delivery, packaging, publicity and all the other things that go into getting a business off the ground. In your plan you should have already stated how long you think this start-up phase will take.

The final timescale you need to take into account is the time it will take to get your product or service to your first customers. This is part of the delivery process mentioned above.

Getting paid

It might be weeks or months before you get money coming into your business. The summary of your cash flow forecast will enable you to work out how long this will take and therefore how much time you need for financial back-up.

After doing a simple break-even analysis you will see how many units or service appointments you have to sell to break even. This, together with your cash flow forecast, will tell you how long it will take you to reach break-even point.

Plan preparation

Make a rough estimate of what you need to do to complete the following and then you can start to create a timetable:

* collect all the information you need – in-house and outside sources
* decide who you need to talk to – people in similar businesses, experts, officials, investors, lenders, grant providers, potential customers
* if you need information from other areas of your business, contact suppliers, long-term customers, partners, employees
* contact the relevant agencies to find out what the requirements are for dealing with tax, insurance, VAT, etc.
* obtain regulatory information for employees and place of work and check certificates are up to date – health and safety, discrimination, maternity leave, etc.
* ensure that your memberships of professional or trade organizations are up to date.

10

writing the plan

Your business plan should be well presented and free from grammatical and spelling mistakes and typos. There are software programs to help you. The content should be logical and the writing jargon-free and clear. Any charts or diagrams should be easy to understand. Supporting materials should be placed in appendices. Keep your plan as short as possible but ensure that it contains all the necessary information. Always include a cover sheet and an executive summary. A basic plan might include the contents page, business profile, marketing plan, operational planning, human resources planning, financial plan and appendices. The exact contents will depend on the size and type of your business. Extra non-paper items can be secured in a pouch or zip bag at the back. Finally check everything for completeness and overlooked mistakes before presenting it. Remember to back up your plan from the computer regularly and keep a spare paper copy.

Producing the plan

There are software programs available that will enable you to complete your business plan on your computer. You can also download business plan forms and sample business plans from the internet. Some firms sell business plan software. Remember that the plans will be generic so be prepared to alter the sample forms and plans to suit your own business. If you are still uncertain about your ability to write the plan you can employ a business plan writer to do it for you.

Most plans will not need to consider the wider implications of privacy and confidentiality, but if your plan is particularly sensitive you might need to ask recipients to sign confidentiality agreements.

Format

When you start to write your plan you need to keep in mind some basic rules about how to write it and set it out. The better looking and easier to read your plan is the more receptive readers will be. That does not mean using lots of fancy typefaces and irrelevant pictures but keeping everything clean and clear.

Use plenty of headings and subheadings to guide your readers and use bullet points and numbered lists where relevant.

Remember the mnemonic KISS: 'Keep it short and simple' or, more direct, 'Keep it simple, stupid!' Remember that you want your plan to be clear and readable. Keep your plan as concise as possible while including all the necessary information. Write it in the third person – do not write 'I' or 'me'; instead use 'the business will …'. Make sure that your writing is straightforward and to the point. Don't use long words or jargon. Only use business or trade specific words if absolutely necessary to explain how your business works. You need to ensure that potential investors or lenders will be able to understand exactly what your business will do and what you hope for financially. You do not want to leave room for any misunderstandings. Once you have written your plan, check it through for spelling and grammar mistakes. *Always* read it on a paper copy, not just on a computer screen. It is far too easy to miss mistakes on a screen. Ideally, ask someone else to read it through for mistakes.

Nothing will irritate your readers more than a document full of spelling and grammatical mistakes or typos. Don't rely on your computer's spellchecker and grammar checker to sort things out. Mistakes are easy to miss on a screen. Also, your spellchecker might pass words that are spelt correctly but are in the wrong place, such as 'is this the write way to the shops?' The spellchecker can be useful for a basic first check through the document, but make sure that it is set to the correct language. In most cases this will be obvious, but British and American English, for example, have different spellings. If you are not confident that your language skills or editing skills are adequate, hire somebody to copy-edit your document for you.

Paper and printing

Do not get too fancy with layout and fonts. The plan should be produced on white A4 paper. Print on one side only and use single spacing. Use a word processor or get somebody else to word process the document. Use black 12 point font in something easy to read, such as Times New Roman. Do not keep changing the font's type or size. You can use underlining or bold to emphasize titles and headings. Use numbered and bullet lists for easy reading where applicable. Supporting documents can be photocopied for inclusion unless the institution you are approaching insists on originals. Number all the pages consecutively from the first page after the cover sheet until the end. Ideally, put your name or the name of your business as a header on each page. This can easily be done in a word-processing program, and it will help readers put the pages back in the correct order if the binding comes loose. Put a blank sheet at the end with your name and address on it and put a clear plastic A4 sheet on the front and back, or use plain card covers. You can bind the document in a simple ring binder or get the document bound at a print shop. There are a variety of simple plastic bindings, such as comb binding or slide binding, that will hold the document together. Do not try to be clever with the presentation. Keep the document portrait format and if you include illustrations or diagrams keep them clear and uncluttered.

How long should it be?

The length of the plan will depend on the type of business, but aim to keep it as short as possible while including all the relevant information. If you produce a plan longer than about 30 pages your readers will fall asleep before they have finished it. On the other hand, if your plan is less than about ten pages long it probably will not contain all the information you need to explain your business. Write the plan to include all the important points but don't add unnecessary details.

Supporting facts and figures

Having worked your way through this book, you will have a lot of information. It is important to keep your writing as succinct as possible but support your arguments with facts and figures wherever possible. Rather than saying, for example, 'There are only a few other companies competing with the proposed business …' write, 'This business will have only three competitors, XYZ, ABC, EFG, who occupy 27% of the present market…'. Make sure that you include the reference for any supporting facts and figures.

Content

The contents of your plan will depend on the type of business, but there are certain items that all plans should contain. You need a cover sheet, executive summary, description of your business, an explanation of who runs it, how it operates and its financial situation as well as any further relevant information.

Cover sheet/title page

This should have the name of your business, your contact details (name, address, phone number, mobile phone number, fax number, email address, web page address). An existing business with a logo could put this on the cover sheet. If you have any partners their names should be listed here. Also if you need to ensure reader confidentiality, this is the place to state the terms. Sometimes a confidentiality form is placed at the beginning of the document and readers are required to sign it.

Also include the period of time the plan covers, for example one year, three years, etc. Include the date that the plan was prepared so that readers can judge how up to date it is.

Contents list

This should include a list of all sections of the plan, including appendices, together with the page numbers. You will write this once the plan has been completed to ensure that the contents page records what is in the document. If you prepare it last you can change the order of the contents without having to rewrite the contents page each time.

Executive summary

This section is often omitted but is actually a vital part of the plan. It is so important that readers in a hurry will only read this part of your plan and might judge your entire plan only on the executive summary. If you omit this section your plan will have little chance of success. It tells the reader what you want. Put this up front so the reader understands exactly why you are presenting the plan. You should use it to record the salient points of each section. The summary should be a clear but succinct précis of the main points of the plan and your argument supporting it.

Description of business/business profile

This section should contain all the necessary information about your business set-up, but as a brief overview.

What you are selling

This is the place to explain exactly what you will be selling. Is it a product or a service? What is its unique selling point (USP)? Why do you think it will sell? How far has it been developed? What feedback have you had about it so far? How does it compare with other competing products or services? What demand is there for your product or service? You need to convince the reader that what you sell will be welcome to potential customers.

Market

Here you describe who you are selling to – your clients or customers – and how you place your product or service in the prevailing market. Explain the results of any market research and quote facts and figures to back up your choice of potential customers. What particular market will your product or service be part of – for example, retail, industrial, financial, service sector, creative? What segment of the market will you be aiming for? Describe the main market trends and identify where your business will fit in, in terms of size, position and segmentation.

Marketing plan

Having explained who your potential customers are you need to explain how you will inform them of what you have to offer. This is where you describe your marketing plan, that is how you will deal with advertising and publicity, what your pricing policy will be and how you will deal with distribution and selling. Even the smallest and most localized business needs to deal with this even if all you intend to do is advertise by word of mouth.

Operations

This should be a précis of your operating system, that is how your business will work on a day-to-day basis. Keep it brief but cover all the main points such as production, premises, materials and suppliers, equipment, staffing, delivery, storage, billing methods and legal and insurance needs.

Management and organization

In this section describe the management system of your business. Explain the key management positions and what they require from managers. If you are the sole owner and have no employees, this section will be brief. Even so, you will need to explain how you intend to deal with running the business and what your strengths are. If there will be deficiencies, explain how your management team will overcome them.

Financial information

This is the place to explain how your business will operate financially. You should include information about the start-up budget and costs of any expansion as well as information about pricing and costing. You need to explain what money it already has and how you hope to raise more. Have you invested your own money in the business? Explain how you will survive financially on a personal level while running the business. You should explain how money will be spent and how you hope to use any new money. Back up your arguments with facts and figures. In essence, it is a summary of the cash flow, forecasting and balance sheets that you prepared earlier and which will be placed in the appendices.

Financial needs

This is why you are preparing the plan. You want money so you need to explain how much you want and when, why and how you want it. You also need to explain how you expect to repay the lender or investor. If you are applying, or have applied, for other kinds of financial assistance, mention them here.

Security

This is linked to the previous section and should be included if relevant. You should give details of your assets. If you are putting your house up as security for a loan, for example, you need to record this.

Appendices

The appendices contain all the supporting information for your plan. If there are many pages to go in the appendices, divide them into appropriate sections. Include in the appendices any official or relevant documents that support the plan, such as rent agreements, professional qualifications or copies of advance orders. This is the place to include originals of documents if required by potential lenders or investors. The appendices should also contain any other relevant information, such as your managers' CVs, a location map of your premises, your financial spreadsheets, and so on. The aim is to make sure that the reader will have all the relevant information to hand so that they can make an informed decision.

Make sure that each page in the appendices is numbered and is clearly labelled so that its purpose is clear. The contents of the appendices should be included on the contents page of the plan so that they can be quickly and easily referred to as the plan is read.

Other items

Lenders or investors might ask for a copy of your plan on disk as well as a paper copy. If you do include non-paper items like these you need to ensure that they are packaged securely with the plan so that they do not get separated from it and lost. Use a transparent pocket with a flap to store a CD or computer disk, or buy special pages that have pockets to hold such items securely and bind them in with the plan.

Back it up!

You shouldn't need reminding to back up your plan from your computer regularly onto a disk. The disk should be stored in a safe place. Not only will this ensure that the latest version of your plan is safe from computer failure but you can easily run off extra copies even if you do not have access to your own computer.

Don't forget the obvious

The final check you should make is to ensure that all the parts of your plan are present before you post it or hand it in. Look at the contents page and then check through the document. It is easy to miss out a section or a vital paragraph. Don't forget to look at the supporting data you have included.

11

using
the plan

Your business plan can be used to apply for financial or other aid and to help you run your business. Before you present your plan, practise giving your presentation at home. When presenting your plan, whether alone or with a partner, be prepared to answer detailed questions about it. If you use visual aids prepare them beforehand and keep them clear and uncluttered and do not try to include too much information on each display page. If the plan is rejected check it, reassess it, rewrite it if necessary and present it again to a new potential investor or lender. If your plan is accepted, use it to monitor the progress of your business. Analyse your plan to find out how well your business is performing against it. Be prepared to change your plan as circumstances change. Use the plan to involve staff and motivate them. Do not give up.

Presenting the plan

You will already have found out whether a potential lender or investor is willing to consider your plan and whether there is a deadline for reaching them. You will have researched, written, checked, assembled and rechecked your plan as advised in Chapter 10. Now you can post it or hand it in so that it arrives by the deadline.

Now you have to wait to see whether you will be asked to take it further by giving a presentation on your plan. What will readers be doing? They will start with the executive summary. Sometimes that is all they will read and your proposal can succeed or fail on that section of the plan alone. If they have time or are interested they might read part or all of the rest of your plan. This initial read of your plan might take anything from a few days to several weeks. You will then be told whether there is enough interest to take it further. If there is, you will probably be asked to meet the readers and present your plan in person and answer any questions they might have.

How the presentation will take place varies. You might simply be asked to discuss your plan further with, for example, your bank manager, or you might be asked to discuss it with several potential lenders or investors. Alternatively, you might be asked to give a full presentation using visual aids.

Whatever the size or type of presentation, you must be prepared to explain your plan in detail and to answer searching questions about any part of it. Expect the questions to be probing and take with you any extra material you need to back up your plan. Read through the plan carefully before the presentation or discussion and try to work out what you might be asked. The financial section is one area that will be discussed in more detail so you need to be sure that you fully understand the financial statements you have included.

Making the presentation

You might make the presentation on your own or with one or more partners. Remember, the boss should always lead any presentation of a business plan – if it is your plan, you must present it. However, if you will be sharing a presentation, your partners can help answer questions on their areas of expertise. Agree beforehand which of you will answer questions on which subjects according to your individual strengths.

On a personal level the interviewers will expect you to be able to discuss your plan clearly and confidently and to be knowledgeable about it. They will also expect you to show enthusiasm for it. If you do not care, why should they? That does not mean jumping up and down and grinning inanely but looking and talking as if you are genuinely excited about what you are offering in the way of a business opportunity.

If you are expected to give a talk and use visual aids make sure that you prepare them well beforehand. Most computer packages nowadays can help you produce a computer based display (Power Point, for example), or you can use flipcharts and markers or handouts. Whichever you use do not make the sheets too ornate or difficult to read. Keep headings large enough to read from the far side of an average room, and keep lists to no more than three to five points. Keep diagrams clear and uncluttered. It is sensible to use handouts even if you are giving a visual aids presentation. They can be used as a reminder by listeners and will help them follow what you are saying.

Do not just read out what is on the screen or board; explain its importance. Make sure that you also refer to the relevant section in your business plan.

After the response

You might get a positive response immediately after a presentation or sometime later after the listeners have had time to discuss your project among themselves. If so, you will be told when the business's financial needs will be met and how this will be done, when to fill the forms in and so on. The response might be that amendments are necessary and the plan will need to be considered again. Before making any changes make sure that you find out exactly why they are necessary and what is required. Then make the changes and resubmit. You might, alas, receive the unwelcome news that your plan has failed to impress anyone. Possibly you might be asked to rewrite and resubmit it, but more likely 'no' will mean just that. If so, look at it long and hard before rewriting or resubmitting it elsewhere. Ask yourself these questions:

1 Is my idea good enough? (Check its USP, market, operational capacity.)

2 Is the idea financially sound? (Check and recheck all the financial figures including the potential market and sales.)

3 Is the idea timely? (Has something similar already been done? Has the idea missed a fashion peak?)

4 Can I really put this plan into operation? (Are managers and staff lined up? Are suppliers and distributors organized? Are premises available?)

5 Did I present my idea in the most clear, logical and persuasive way? (Check for basic mistakes, organization of sections, presentation of document, adequate supporting evidence.)

6 Did I approach the right people for help? (Do you need a lender or investor? Are there people who could provide other kinds of help?)

7 Did I fail to impress people at the presentation? (Do you need practice in public speaking? A partner at the presentation? Did you lack enthusiasm?)

Assuming that you have answered all these questions and have rechecked and rewritten the plan in the light of any new research necessary, submit it to someone else. The millionaires of today are the people who never gave up.

The way forward

There are several ways in which your business plan will help you run your business. It can be a guide to where you want to get to as well as a vehicle for communicating within the organization. It will do these things:

* show the way forward
* monitor performance

* assess achievements and weaknesses
* co-ordinate control
* help communication
* empower staff
* generate ideas.

Once you have finished the plan it comes into its own as a way of monitoring the direction your business will take. You should be constantly comparing what your business is actually doing with how you envisaged it in the plan. There may be times when the business is going in a different direction to the plan, in which case you need to bring it back into line or be able to justify such a change. If business is down and you are not keeping to the plan, you can look at the plan and see where you are going wrong. The plan will change according to the changes you make in the company and it will need to be rewritten every year taking into account necessary changes.

One way of using the plan is to subject it to SWOT analysis (see Chapter 3). This is a useful technique for analysing your product or service. However, it can also be used to analyse the plan, and therefore your business, as a whole. Using your business plan as a starting point, analyse it by listing problems and achievements under the four SWOT headings. Use the SWOT analysis regularly. It is useful not only as you start to put the plan into action, but also as your business changes and progresses.

Use your plan to monitor performance and manage it. By comparing regularly what you are doing with what you wrote in your plan, you can see where performance needs to be improved or changed. Use the plan to set short- and long-term objectives for individual staff and the business as a whole.

Use your plan to ensure that every manager at whatever level in the business knows what should be done and has written guidance about the time each stage should take and who should be doing what. It will also help your managers to understand what time and cost limitations there are so that they can work within them. The plan can be the basis of regular meetings to fine-tune or change the plan so that everyone in the business is working to the same blueprint. Control therefore becomes co-ordinated and effective.

By ensuring that everyone in the business sees the plan and understands how it will be put into practice you empower your staff and make them feel part of the business. This motivates them and helps retain staff who feel valued and included. The plan can clarify to everyone what should be happening and leaves less room for mistakes or misunderstandings. An initial meeting to discuss the plan can be beneficial in ensuring your employees' co-operation.

If staff are aware of the expectations for the business you can rely on them more to work in ways that will benefit the company. A clear understanding of the situation and expectations allows you to give more leeway to staff to take their own decisions. With regular reporting back and clear guidance based on the plan, your staff can be empowered to make decisions at their level and thus leave you with more time to concentrate on the overall picture.

Once the plan has been written and the business is operating along the lines laid out in the plan it can encourage new ways of thinking from managers and other employees. Staff reading the plan and relating it to their work might think of better ways of doing their jobs, new uses for equipment or innovations in customer service, for example. Ideas can be triggered by reading the plan, which is why it is important that it is used to aid communication amongst staff. Comparing what actually happens to what is written down can create discussion and innovative thinking. The people doing the work are the best people to find new and improved ways of doing things. Encourage responses to the plan, not just when it first comes into use but regularly along the way.